WILD WILTSHIRE

A celebration of the wildlife and living landscapes of Wiltshire

Wiltshire Wildlife Trust

Wiltshire Wildlife Trust is a registered Charity No: 266202.
Incorporated as a company limited by guarantee with No: 73056.
Registered Office: Elm Tree Court, Long Street, Devizes, Wiltshire, SN10 1NJ. Tel: 01380 725670

INTRODUCTION FROM OUR SPONSOR

The Hills Group is extremely proud of its long standing partnership with the Wiltshire Wildlife Trust. This book is a celebration of Wiltshire's amazing wildlife and the natural environment that our long standing partnership supports and continues to protect.

This successful partnership started in 1990 and since then we have worked together to create wildlife rich habitats that sustain the county's biodiversity. It is a key aim of the partnership to provide the public with access to the wonders of Wiltshire's countryside and the opportunity to enjoy, explore and learn about all that it has to offer.

The Hills Group takes its environmental responsibilities seriously and we look forward to continuing the important work done together with the Wiltshire Wildlife Trust. At Hills we are committed to giving something back for the benefit of all communities in Wiltshire. Supporting the Wiltshire Wildlife Trust ensures that wildlife habitats are not only created but are also protected for future generations to enjoy.

We hope this book will inspire its readers to visit and experience first-hand the ever changing beauty of the Wiltshire landscapes and the diverse wildlife it supports.

Mike Hill
Chief Executive, The Hills Group

Text Copyright © Wiltshire Wildlife Trust 2016.
Rights: Images © Contributing photographers.

Design and production: Nick Otway.
Image retouching and colour repro: Michael Moody.

A catalogue record for this book is available from the British Library.

ISBN: 978-0-9566215-1-1

Printed and bound in Italy by Printer Trento S.r.l.

www.wiltshirewildlife.org

FOREWORD

Welcome to this celebration of Wiltshire's wildlife. The extraordinary images in this book illustrate the incredible beauty and variety of our county. Taking us on a tour through the County's Living Landscapes, this book reminds us of why Wiltshire is such a special place.

Through the photographers' lens we can look in wonder and delight at Wiltshire's landscapes, habitats and species. From scenes of misty mornings to the microscopic detail of insects, these images reveal a world of nature that sometimes only those with an artistic eye can see.

Over the past few years my passion for nature has been enhanced by a renewed interest in wildlife photography. The photos in this book demonstrate the fruits of many patient hours spent waiting for the sun to rise or for an animal or bird to appear. We are delighted to have worked with some of the county's best, but perhaps unknown wildlife photographers. Their stunning images are shared here for us all to enjoy and take inspiration from.

Gary Mantle
Chief Executive, Wiltshire Wildlife Trust

CONTENTS

Living Landscapes

World famous sites such as Stonehenge and Avebury remind us that Wiltshire has a long and ancient history. The relationship of geology, climate, wildlife and people has, over thousands of years, given us a rich tapestry of living landscapes shaped by farming and the pattern of development.

Wildlife has always lived alongside and adapted to the rhythm and changing patterns of land use. Wildlife in Wiltshire has broadly adapted to two distinct landscape types, and their associated habitats. The phrase 'as different as chalk and cheese' comes from a description of the two main geological and hence farming areas within Wiltshire.

The 'chalk' forms the rolling downlands of Salisbury Plain, West Wiltshire and the Marlborough Downs and covers about two thirds of the county. Wiltshire has forty per cent of all the chalk in the UK and remarkably the UK has eighty per cent of all the chalk found in the world. The downland turf is one of the richest habitats and a square metre can contain as many as forty different species of plant, including many different kinds of orchid. Flowing from the chalk aquifers, the crystal clear streams and rivers are like jewels in Wiltshire's crown and are home to a greater variety of wildlife than any other type of river in Britain.

The 'cheese' comes from the gently undulating farmland which lies on the upper Jurassic clays in the north and west of the county; the Braydon Forest and Avon Vale areas. The ancient forests that once covered Britain were hard to clear on these heavy clay soils, as was the cultivation of crops. The area is rich in woods and hedges, and home to many species of birds, bats and butterflies, as well as many 'veteran' trees. Ponds and ditches add to the diversity of habitats. Hay meadows were once a common sight but over ninety seven percent have disappeared due to agricultural intensification. The finest surviving hay meadows in Britain are found in Wiltshire. The colours of the myriad of flowers, and the stirring sound of insects and birds are a reminder of what we have lost.

This book is divided into broadly distinctive Living Landscape areas. Within each area occurs a rich and varied wildlife. Though wildlife has declined, fortunately the wildlife losses within Wiltshire have generally been less severe than in some other parts of the UK. This book celebrates the wildlife within, and the beauty of these landscapes. It reminds us all of what we still have, and also what we face losing if we don't work together towards a more sustainable future for wildlife and people. To thrive in the future, wildlife sites need to be bigger, better managed, better connected and buffered from the impacts of adjacent land uses. Wiltshire Wildlife Trust works actively to achieve this, and looks forward to the future working with others to improve the fortunes of wildlife and people throughout Wiltshire and Swindon.

Location of our nature reserves

A map of the Living Landscapes of Wiltshire and Swindon showing the location of Wiltshire Wildlife Trust nature reserves.

Wiltshire Upper Thames Clay Vale
1. Upper Waterhay
2. Lower Moor Farm
   including Clattinger Farm,
   Sandpool, Oaksey Moor Farm Meadow

Swindon Ridge and Clay Lowlands
1. Hagbourne Copse
2. Rushey Platt
3. St Julian's Community
   Woodland
4. Swindon Lagoons

Braydon Forest
1. The Firs
2. Echo Lodge Meadows
3. Blakehill Farm and
   Stoke Common
   Meadows
4. Cloatley Meadows
5. Emmett Hill Meadows
6. Ravensroost Wood
   including Ravensroost
   and Avis Meadows, and
   Distillery and Warbler
   Meadows

Cotswolds Limestone Lowlands
1. Vincients Wood

Marlborough Downs and Savernake Forest
1. High Clear Down
2. Hat Gate
3. Ramsbury Meadow
4. Clouts Wood including
   Markham Banks, Kings Farm
   Wood, Diocese Meadows
5. Morgan's Hill

Bristol Avon Vale
1. Green Lane Wood
   including Biss Wood
   and Green Lane
   Nature Park
2. Conigre Mead
3. Penn Wood
4. Widbrook Wood

Vale of Pewsey
1. Jones's Mill
   (the Vera
   Jeans Reserve)
2. Ham Hill
3. Peppercombe
   Wood
4. Devizes and Roundway
   Orchard and Old Cricket Field

Salisbury Plain
1. The Devenish
2. Cockey Down
3. Dunscombe Bottom

Warminster and the Vale of Wardour
1. Oysters Coppice
2. Smallbrook Meadows

West Wiltshire and Cranborne Chase Downs
1. Langford Lakes
2. Coombe Bissett Down
3. Middleton Down
4. Little Langford Down
5. Nadder Island

Tytherley and Langley Woods
1. Blackmoor Copse (the Vaughan-Pickard Reserve)
2. Landford Bog

The Braydon Forest and The Cotswold Water Park

Lying between Malmesbury in the west and Swindon to the east is an area traditionally known as the **Braydon Forest**. This is a varied landscape of mature woodlands and traditionally managed pastures (used for grazing) and meadows (where the hay is cut for winter fodder). These grassland habitats support a rich mix of wild flowers and grasses which in turn support a large variety of insects: bees, hoverflies, butterflies, moths, and song birds and bats. These meadows, pastures, ponds and hedgerows can be explored at Trust nature reserves such as Distillery Farm Meadows, Cloatley Meadows, Stoke Common Meadows, Emmett Hill and Echo Lodge.

Woodland management over the centuries has created and maintained varied habitats such as high tree canopies, sunny glades and woodland margins, sustaining a wide range of wildlife which can be seen at Ravensroost Wood and The Firs nature reserves. Historically the woodlands had large, mature trees with an understory generally of hazel which was coppiced. Large trees provided timber for building, and the coppiced understory provided thinner poles for fencing, wattle, tools and firewood.

At the very north of the county lies the southern part of the **Cotswold Water Park** at the head of the Thames Valley. Since the Second World War there has been extensive gravel extraction for road and building construction which has in turn left a patchwork of lakes in the flat landscape. The resulting pits and margins have been developed and managed in different ways to produce a variety of uses and habitats. Some of these lakes are important breeding, resting and overwintering places for wildfowl, including nationally important populations of tufted duck, pochard, gadwall and great crested grebe. Around the lakes are reed beds providing homes for rare and elusive bitterns and reed warblers.

On the edge of the Water Park, Clattinger Farm supports the most extensive species rich hay meadows in England. This unique lowland farm is the only lowland English farm to have never received any artificial agricultural chemicals. That and its traditional grazing and hay cutting management have created and sustained the flower-rich meadows, full of snake's head fritillaries, orchids, and many other beautiful wild flowers. These meadows are grazed by the Trust's herd of Belted Galloway cattle.

SNAKE'S-HEAD FRITILLARIES *Fritllaria meleagris*
CLATTINGER FARM
STEPHEN DAVIS

This beautiful flower is native to floodplain meadows in north Wiltshire. Only thirty such meadows remain in the UK, with six in Wiltshire.

GREEN-WINGED ORCHIDS *Orchis morio* AND COWSLIPS *Primula veris*
(ABOVE)
CLATTINGER FARM
ROBERT HARVEY

After the wonderful display of snake's head fritillaries in April, green-winged orchids are the first orchid to emerge. They become abundant alongside cowslips during May, occurring in their thousands.

BURNT ORCHID *Orchis ustulata* (RIGHT)
CLATTINGER FARM
STEPHEN DAVIS

More commonly a species of chalk downland, this nationally rare species occasionally occurs in species rich hay meadows such as at Clattinger Farm. Wiltshire is a national stronghold for this striking orchid which has declined dramatically in other counties.

SOUTHERN MARSH ORCHID *Dactylorhiza praetermissa* **(LEFT)**
CLATTINGER FARM
ROBERT HARVEY

Southern marsh orchids occur in the damper wet channels which cut across the meadows at Clattinger Farm. They flower alongside early marsh *Dactylorhiza incarnata* and common spotted *Dactylorhiza fuchsii* orchids. These (Dactylorhiza) species all hybridize with each other, leading to a great variety of colour and form within a single field.

GREEN-WINGED ORCHIDS *Orchis morio* **(ABOVE)**
Clattinger Farm
STEPHEN DAVIS

A beautiful early spring orchid. Historically common in traditional hay meadows, it can occur in great abundance.

DEVIL'S-BIT SCABIOUS *Succisa pratensis* AND DROPWORT *Fillipendula vulgaris* **(ABOVE)**
HAY MEADOW, CLATTINGER FARM
STEPHEN DAVIS

Wiltshire supports some of the finest remaining hay meadows in England. In July the blue flashes of devil's-bit scabious, and soft creams of dropwort and meadowsweet *Filipendula ulmaria* provide a final flash of colour before the hay is cut.

COMMON SPOTTED ORCHID *Dactylorhiza fuchsii* **(RIGHT)**
CLATTINGER FARM
STEPHEN DAVIS

Common spotted orchids follow in June and occur in their tens of thousands in the meadows at Clattinger Farm. They occur in a great variety of colour form, from pure white, through to pink and purple.

HAWKBITS AND TREFOILS
SIDE HAM, CLATTINGER FARM
STEPHEN DAVIS

The flowering season progresses through a succession of colour phases. Deep reds of nodding snake's-head fritillaries, abundant in April, are replaced by the yellows of cowslips *Primlua veris*, hawkbits and trefoils. June arrives with whites of Oxeye daisies *Leucanthemum vulgare*, interspersed with the pink spears of common spotted orchids *Dactylorhiza fuschii*. Finally the meadows are awash with the deep reds and purples of knapweed *Centaurea nigra*, betony *Stachys officinalis* and sawwort *Serratula tinctoria*.

GREAT BURNETT *Sanguisorba officinalis*
CLATTINGER FARM
STEPHEN DAVIS

Great Burnett is a characteristic indicator of floodplain meadows, and is historically common in meadows within the Thames valley. Only fifteen hundred hectares of floodplain meadow habitat remain in England. Great Burnett is abundant in several meadows at Clattinger Farm and is successfully being restored to the meadows at Blakehill Farm.

ROE DEER *Capreolus capreolus*
TADPOLE FARM NATURE PARK
STEPHEN DAVIS

Forty hectares of restored floodplain meadows are being created on arable
land at Tadpole Farm, adjacent to the River Ray, to the south of Cricklade.
After two years the meadows are already enjoyed by roe deer *Capreolus
capreolus* and brown hare *Lepus europaeus*.

NORTH MEADOW NATIONAL NATURE RESERVE, WINTER FLOOD
CRICKLADE
PHIL SELBY

North Meadow at Cricklade supports eighty percent of the UK
population of snake's head fritillary. A classic floodplain meadow,
bounded by both the river Thames and the river Churn. While floods
are normal North Meadow has experienced prolonged winter and
spring flooding in recent years.

GREY HERON *Ardea cinerea*
LOWER MOOR FARM
PHILIP MALE

A very successful species the grey heron can often be seen fishing at the water's edge of any river, canal, lake or pond, including garden ponds. Herons gather together to nest in communal heronries high in the tree tops. There is a large heronry at the Trust's Lower Moor Farm nature reserve in the Cotswold Water Park.

MUTE SWAN *Cygnus olor*
LOWER MOOR FARM
PHILIP MALE

The mute swan occurs widely across Witlshire's wetlands and river valleys, with particular concentrations in the Cotswolds Water Park and the major rivers such as the river Avon. It is also a common sight on larger town and country ponds, and canals.

OTTER *Lutra lutra*
LOWER MOOR FARM
PHIL SELBY

Otters can be seen at the Trust's nature reserves at Lower Moor Farm and Langford Lakes. We know they are successfully breeding, and families with two cubs are regularly seen.

WATER VOLE *Arvicola amphibious*
SWINDON LAGOONS
STEVE DEELEY

The water vole is Britain's fastest declining mammal. Wiltshire is a relative
stronghold for this species where it occurs along rivers, streams and ditches,
and around ponds.

DOWNY EMERALD *Cordulia aenea* DRAGONFLY
LOWER MOOR FARM
STEVE COVEY

A scarce dragonfly, this species prefers tree lined woodland ponds, lakes and canals. It is one of the first species to emerge in early May. It is poor at dispersing, preferring a life foraging along the edge of the woodland canopy. It was first recorded in the Water Park as recently as 1989.

ROE DEER *Capreolus capreolus*
SWALLOW POOL, LOWER MOOR FARM
PHIL SELBY

Roe deer are regularly seen in and around the hay meadows of Clattinger
Farm and Lower Moor Farm. It seems that a preferred short cut sometimes
includes a swim across the lake. Up to four deer have been seen crossing
together.

BULLFINCHES *Pyrrhula pyrrhula* **(LEFT)**
LOWER MOOR FARM
STEVE DEELEY

The striking bullfinch is associated mostly with wooded areas in Wiltshire including the Braydon Forest, the Cotswolds, Savernake, the Vale of Wardour, Bentley Wood and within the New Forest. It is largely absent from the Marlborough Downs and Salisbury Plain.

KINGFISHER *Alcedo atthis* **(ABOVE)**
LOWER MOOR FARM
PHIL SELBY

There are few greater thrills than seeing a kingfisher. Often preceeded by a sharp shrill 'peep' followed by a blue flash, the kingfisher is perhaps best seen from a hide or sheltered spot, where fishing can be observed relatively easily, as the bird returns regularly to the same perch before diving to catch its prey.

MALLARD LAKE
LOWER MOOR FARM
STEPHEN DAVIS

Originally the result of gravel digging, the shallow lakes in the Cotswold Water Park are nationally important for their specialist water plant community. Deposits of calcium carbonate (or marl) provide these clear waters with a distinctive aquatic plant community, rich in stoneworts (*Chara* species) and pondweeds (*Potamogeton* species). The lakes are also nationally important for wetland birds, including, smew *Mergellus arbellus*, coot *Fulica atra*, tufted duck *Aythya fuligula*, pochard *Aythya ferina*, gadwall *Anas strepera*, shoveler *Anas clypeata* and great crested grebe *Podiceps cristatus*.

POCHARD *Aythya ferina*
COTSWOLD WATER PARK
PHILIP MALE

Cotswold Water Park supports nationally important wintering populations
of pochard. A very rare occasional breeding bird in Wiltshire, peak numbers
occur in winter with birds migrating from the colder climates of Scandinavia
and eastern Europe.

GREAT CRESTED GREBE *Podiceps cristatus*
COTSWOLD WATER PARK
PHILIP MALE

Cotswold Water Park supports nationally important populations of great crested grebe. This most elegant of birds has benefited from the creation of shallow lakes in the water park, where it favours relatively large bodies of open still water with emergent vegetation and a plentiful supply of fish. Great crested grebe were almost persecuted to extinction in the UK because their feathers were highly prized.

BROWN HAIRSTREAK BUTTERFLY, MALE *Thecla betulae*
RAVENSROOST WOOD
STEVE COVEY

This is a secretive butterfly which emerges late in the season, in August.
A resident of a landscape rich in thick blackthorn *Prunus spinosa* hedges,
thickets, and woodland rides. The female lays her eggs on blackthorn twigs
often at the junction of a spine and a twig. They spend much of their time
in the canopy, feeding on aphid honeydew. They will descend to feed on
brambles, thistles and hemp argimony *Eupatorium cannabinum*. Relatively
common in the Braydon Forest but hard to see high in the canopy.

COPPICE WITH STANDARDS
RAVENSROOST WOOD
STEPHEN DAVIS

Ravensroost Wood is an ancient remnant of the medieval Royal Hunting
Forest of Braydon. Parts have been under continuous woodland cover
since at least 1600. The Trust has re-introduced the practice of coppicing,
promoting a diverse range of trees, flowers, birds and insects. The wood is
designated as a Site of Special Scientific Interest (SSSI). The edges of the
rides are abundant with wildflowers, primrose *Primlua vulgaris*, violets *Viola
canina*, early purple *orchis mascula*, common spotted *Dactylorhiza fushii*
and greater butterfly *Platanthera chlorantha* orchids.

GRASS SNAKE *Natrix natrix*
RAVENSROOST WOOD
STEVE COVEY

The UK's largest snake is often called the water snake, it actively preys on frogs and toads, but will also take small birds and mammals. It can be found in the proximity of ponds, slow flowing rivers and canals. The grass snake lays eggs, sometimes in garden compost heaps which offer a warm environment to incubate the eggs.

ADDER *Viperus berus*
BLAKEHILL FARM
STEVE COVEY

The adder is the UK's only venomous snake. Adders usually eat small rodents such as voles and mice. They will eat lizards, frogs and newts, and will also take young birds from the nests of ground nesting birds. Unlike the grasssnake the adder gives birth to live young.

Swindon Ridge and Clay Lowlands

The Borough of Swindon has by far the largest concentration of people and industry. About a third of the total Wiltshire and Swindon population live within the borough. The small village on the hill, with its distinctive grey stone, grew through the development of the railway works, (the site was chosen and visited by Isambard Kingdom Brunel) and latterly, through other transport industries, such as car manufacture, to its present size. Today the town has a wide variety of industries and several companies and organisations have relocated to Swindon from London.

Within the town there are parks, gardens, lakes and open public spaces with natural corridors, paths, cycleways and rivers. Some recently built housing estates have kept old hedgerows and mature trees; open grassy tracts with trees are a feature of many estates. Larger areas with copses, grassland, ponds and marshy sections run like green fingers through to the Old Town. With hedgerow birds and roe deer commonly seen, these zones bring the countryside into the heart of the town. Some of these areas are actively managed for wildlife. At any time of the year these are variously used for exercise, recreation and engaging with wildlife.

Coate Water, on Swindon's doorstep, was originally built as a reservoir for the nearby canals and has, over the years, become home to wildlife as well as a place of recreation. Just south of the main lake at Coate is a restricted area containing a heronry.

The water quality and bank side habitats of the river Ray and remaining pieces of canal have greatly improved over recent years and otters returned to Swindon before some other parts of Wiltshire. One nature reserve within the town is Rushey Platt, a fen-like marsh near the river Ray and Kingshill canal. Hagbourne Copse nature reserve is a mature stand of oak standards and hazel coppice. Roe deer are often seen in the open wildlife areas of Swindon and also live in Hagbourne Copse. The large red kites, with their distinctive forked tails, are occasionally seen high over the buildings, having spread from the re-introduced population in the Chilterns.

WINTER
WILTS AND BERKS CANAL
PHIL SELBY

The Wilts and Berks canal provides a wetland corridor within the new developments in south Swindon at Wichelstowe.

MALLARD *Anas platyrhynchos*
WILTS AND BERKS CANAL, SWINDON
PHIL SELBY

Perhaps our most familiar duck species due to its presence on town ponds.
Mallard breed throughout Wiltshire and there are thought to be more than
fifteen hundred breeding pairs. These are supplemented by birds from
Europe during the winter with up to six thousands birds occurring.

LITTLE EGRET *Egretta garzetta*
SWINDON LAGOONS
STEVE DEELEY

The little egret, a member of the heron family, has only recently colonised southern England as a breeding bird. Its appearance is thought to be an indicator of a warming climate as birds spread north from southern Europe. The little egret was first recorded in Wiltshire in 1992, and is now a relatively common site in the Cotswold Water Park and on the River Avon and its tributaries. In winter roosts of up to thirty birds have been recorded.

STARLING MURMURATION *Sturnus vulgaris*
SWINDON
PHIL SELBY

Starlings will gather as large winter roosts, even in semi-urban situations
where suitable habitat occurs, such as here in reed beds in Swindon.

COATE WATER SUNSET
COATE WATER
PHILIP MALE

Coate Water was originally built as a feeder lake for the Wilts and Berks canal. It is now one of the most important sites in Wiltshire for breeding reed warblers *Acrocephalus scirpaceus* and great crested grebe *Podiceps cristatus*. The lake is also important for many wintering waterbirds and attracts waders on passage during migration. It also supports an outstanding assemblage of fifteen species of dragonfly and damselfly.

HERON *Ardea cinerea*
WILTS AND BERKS CANAL
PHIL SELBY

The grey heron is a successful wetland species, which occupies a great diversity of wetland habitats. These include most of Wiltshire's rivers, lakes, ponds and canals, where it feeds on fish, amphibians, insects, reptiles and even small birds.

BLUEBELLS *Hyacinthoides non-scripta*
HAGBOURNE COPSE NATURE RESERVE
STEPHEN DAVIS

Hagbourne Copse survives as a remnant of ancient woodland comprising oak *Quercus robur* standards and hazel *Corylus avellana* coppice. Surrounded by an industrial estate and the M4 motorway it was formerly part of the Lydiard Estate, having been planted over two hundred and fifty years ago. While only two hectares in size it supports an abundance of wildlife including great spotted wood peckers *Dendrocopos major*, tawny owl *Strix aluco* and purple hairstreak *Favonius quercus* butterflies.

LYDIARD PARK WINTER
LYDIARD PARK
PHIL SELBY

In addition to the Palladian house the beautiful historic estate of Lydiard
Park supports a diversity of habitats including two lakes. Here a variety
of waterfowl such as coot *Fulica atra*, moorhen *Gallinula chloropus*, great
crested grebe *Podiceps cristatus*, tufted duck *Aythya fuligula*, mallard *Anas
platyrhynchos* and little grebe *Tachybaptus ruficollis* can be seen.

LYDIARD PARK SNOWDROPS *Galanthus nivalis*
LYDIARD PARK
PHIL SELBY

Snowdrops flower in late winter, often as early as January, in parks and gardens. However the snowdrop is also naturalised within many Wiltshire hedgerows, lanes and woodlands.

ROE DEER *Capreolus capreolus*
WICHELSTOWE
PHIL SELBY

Roe Deer are often seen in pastures and woodlands including, as here, on the urban fringe of Swindon at Wichelstowe. Wiltshire towns often enjoy a swift transition between urban and rural habitats.

REED BUNTING *Emberiza schoeniclus*
COATE WATER
ROBERT HARVEY

A species that favours river valleys and fringes of open water for breeding.
The reed bunting likes to feed in winter on the seeds of grasses and herbs,
especially farmland weeds.

WAXWING *Bombycilla garrulus*
WROUGHTON
PHILIP MALE

This very attractive bird is a rare winter visitor which doesn't breed in the
UK. Winter irruptions occur when a failure in rowan *Sorbus aucuparia* berry
crops in northern Europe coincides with a population peak. Birds will
then migrate from Scandinavia to seek food. Flocks will quickly strip even
urban trees of berries as here in the car park of the Ellendune Centre in
Wroughton.

The Cotswolds

To the north west of the county the landscape is typical of the southern **Cotswolds**. Stretching north from Bradford-on-Avon, through Box and up past Castle Combe, this is an area of rolling, open plateaus with steep, interlocking, hidden valleys and is part of the Cotswolds Area of Outstanding Natural Beauty. The plateau has extensive arable farming with widespread farms and lonely barns. Patches of woodland dot the plateau and woodland hangers hug the coombe sides.

During spring and summer, butterflies flit amongst the flowers which pattern the small fields of these quiet valleys, whilst buzzards soar and call above. In the evenings the air is home to a variety of bats gliding and swooping as they hunt the darting moths. The area is known for these populations of bats, ranging from the common pipistrelle to the much rarer greater horseshoe bat. The thin layer of soil on the coombe sides is poor in nutrients which are constantly leached down through the porous bedrock by rain. This, however, results in a rich variety of flowering plants such as cowslips, orchids, rockroses and vetches.

Some of the latter are fed on by the caterpillars of several species of butterflies particularly the chalkhill and adonis blues. Often the valley sides are too steep for tractors and so have escaped the application of man-made fertilisers, keeping the rich mix of vegetation and associated creatures. These grassland and scrub areas provide food and nesting places for many birds throughout the year, such as spotted flycatchers and green woodpeckers, whilst flocks of redwings and fieldfares find food and shelter during the winter months.

Running through this area is the Bybrook, a crystal clear calciferous stream broadening into a river as it flows south. The stream is home to much wildlife and is particularly noted for the rare crustacean, the white-clawed crayfish, which looks like a miniature lobster. Otters have returned to the Bybrook after being absent for many years. The dipper is a relatively frequent sight, bobbing on rocks before disappearing underwater, as it searches for insects in the cool water.

Wool and cloth manufacture were traditional industries in the Cotswolds. Many of the traditional stone cottages of the small towns and picturesque villages were the homes and workplaces of spinners and weavers. The cottage walls and roofs were built with the local oolitic limestone fashioned into appropriate stone blocks and tiles, characteristic of the Cotswolds. These days the area supports farming, and tourism is increasingly important.

WILD GARLIC *Allium ursinum* ANCIENT OAKS *Quercus robur*
CASTLE COMBE
STEPHEN DAVIS

The valley sides of the Bybrook contain both limestone grassland and areas of woodland. Wild garlic carpets the woodland floor in spring in the woodlands to the south of Castle Combe.

CHALKHILL BLUE *Lysandra coridon* AND CARLINE THISTLE *Carlina vulgaris* (**ABOVE**)
WEST YATTON DOWN
STEPHEN DAVIS

The chalkhill blue is an absolutely characteristic butterfly of the limestone grasslands that occur on the steep valley sides of the coombes that incise the limestone plateau. It breeds on the small legume horseshoe vetch *Hippocrepis comosa* which is confined to lime rich soils that occur in Wiltshire. Carline thistle is a favoured nectar source.

COMMON BLUE *Polyommatus icarus* (**RIGHT**)
COTSWOLDS
ROBERT HARVEY

The common blue is sadly not so common nowadays. Breeding on birdsfoot trefoil *Lotus corniculatus*, it occurs on chalk downlands and the limestone grasslands of the Cotswolds. It also occurs in other grassland habitats where the food plant grows, such as hay meadows and pastures and also more sensitively managed road verges.

BARN SWALLOW *Hirundo rustica* **(LEFT)**
COTSWOLDS
STEVE DEELEY

One of the classic signs of spring which many people wait for, is the return of the swallow from its wintering grounds in southern Africa. They are relatively widely distributed in Wiltshire and are most often seen swooping low over pasture where livestock are grazed, catching their insect prey.

DIPPER *Cinclus cinclus* **(ABOVE)**
BYBROOK STREAM
JAMES FISHER

The Dipper is a remarkable small passerine, characterised by its habit of walking under the surface of fast flowing streams where it seeks out its invertebrate prey. It nests at the water's edge in amongst tree roosts, rock crevices or gaps within man-made structures such as bridges. The Bybrook stream is the Wiltshire stronghold for this species, thought to support between fifteen and twenty breeding pairs.

FIELD MAPLES *Acer campestre* AND WILD GARLIC *Allium ursinum*
(ABOVE)
RACK HILL
STEPHEN DAVIS

The fluted bark of large ancient field maples are a characteristic feature of the woodlands on the valley slopes above the Bybrook. Field maple prefers the alakaline soils which are generated on the oolitic limestone of the area.

PYRAMIDAL ORCHID *Anacamptis pyramidalis* **(RIGHT)**
RACK HILL
STEPHEN DAVIS

The pyramidal orchid is abundant on both the limestone and chalk grasslands of Wiltshire. Usually in full flower in late June and July they are very often pollinated by six-spot burnet *Zygaena filipendulae* and five-post burnet *Zygaena trifolii* moths. These beautiful day flying moths both breed on birds foot trefoil *Lotus corniculatus*.

BEE ORCHID *Ophrys apifera* **(LEFT)**
WEST YATTON DOWN
STEPHEN DAVIS

The bee orchid is very striking in the way the flower mimics a bee. This is an evolutionary strategy to fool and attract pollinating insects. In actual fact, most bee orchids in the UK are self pollinated. Here the clearly visible pollen sac can be seen. They occur often as single plants or in small groups, on limestone and chalk grassland, wherever conditions are favourable, including some road verges.

GREY WAGTAIL *Motacilla cinerea* **(ABOVE)**
BYBROOK
PHILP MALE

Of the three wagtail species occuring in Wiltshire, this species is the most closely associated with water preferring fast flowing streams and rivers such as the Bybrook. The winter distribution is different when this species expands its range to include more open farmland, farmyards and even urban centres including many towns.

Bristol Avon Vale

The Bristol Avon Vale includes a large area of relatively flat clay lowlands (the cheese as opposed to the chalk). This large catchment extends south of Malmesbury towards Trowbridge. The Bristol Avon is a large clay river which drains this catchment and is prone to periodic flash flooding. The river can rise several metres in a short time after periods of high rainfall. This can cause localised flooding.

Drifts of creamy coloured meadowsweet and deep blue meadow cranesbill characterise the damp soils at Conigre Mead nature reserve on the banks of the River Avon. Within the town of Melksham this reserve is a valuable haven for wildlife and is home to many dragonfly and damselfy species.

Green Lane Wood and Biss Wood nature reserves are two wonderful ancient woodlands where many oak and ash standards occur above a hazel understory. Areas of high forest support rare bat populations, such as the Bechstein's bat. Both woods are renowned for their woodland flowers, butterflies and many fungi. Primroses and violets carpet the woodland floor in spring.

Ancient woodlands are those areas that have been continuously wooded for at least the last six hundred years, possibly millenia, and consequently they generally have a large diversity of flowering plants, ferns, mosses and fungi. This native flora supports a great diversity of insects and other invertebrates, as they and the plants have evolved together. The plants and creatures provide food for birds and other animals such as deer, badgers and voles. Man has, over centuries, managed the woodlands and they contain different structural layers and habitats. In these woods the tree canopy usually comprises oak with ash, field maple and the occasional wild cherry, with alder and aspen in wetter areas.

The lower shrub layers are predominantly hazel along with dogwood, hawthorn and holly. The reserves and other woods in the area are home to many woodland birds such as great spotted woodpeckers, jays and the smaller nuthatches and tree creepers. Many fungi and some invertebrates, particularly a few rare beetles, need dying and rotting wood to complete their life cycles. Commonly seen fungi are the black lumps on ash, aptly named as King Alfred's Cakes. Less common are lilac coloured wood blewits and speckled topped blushers. Vast numbers of millipedes, snails and woodlice live in the leaf litter where they breakdown and recycle dead plant and animal material.

ANCIENT COPPICE STOOLS OF ASH *Fraxinus excelsior,* AND FIELD
MAPLE *Acer campestre*
BISS WOOD
STEPHEN DAVIS

Biss Wood is an outstanding fragment of ancient woodland to the east of
Trowbridge. Centuries of coppice management are evidenced by many old
oak and field maple coppice stools. Many have rot holes and features that
support nesting birds and roosting bats.

BROAD-BODIED CHASER, FEMALE *Libellula depressa*
GREEN LANE WOOD
STEVE COVEY

A common species that favours small open ponds and which colonises new
ponds very quickly, including garden ponds.

SILVER-WASHED FRITILLARY, FEMALE *Argynnis paphia*
GREEN LANE WOOD
STEVE COVEY

Our largest fritillary occurs in mature oak woods rich in violets growing on
the woodland floor. Eggs are laid on the north side of a mossy tree trunk.
The hatched larvae descend to the woodland floor to feed on common dog
violet *Viola canina*.

VIEW ACROSS THE VALE TO ROUNDWAY DOWN, FROM BROMHAM
(ABOVE)
ROUNDWAY DOWN
STEPHEN DAVIS

November sunrise looking across the vale back towards the scarp slope of
Roundway Down.

PRIMROSE *Primula vulgaris* **(RIGHT)**
BISS WOOD
STEPHEN DAVIS

Primroses carpet the woodland floor in early spring before the canopy
closes, responding to the increased light levels following coppice
management.

BROWN HARE *Lepus europaeus*
BROADTOWN
PHILIP MALE

A declining species of farmland, Wiltshire is a relative stronghold for the
brown hare, where it occurs on open downland and meadows. Young
leverets are born fully formed with eyes open, and rest up above ground in
a shallow depression within the grassland sward.

GREAT SPOTTED WOOD PECKER *Dendrocopos major*
BROADTOWN
PHILIP MALE

The most common of the UK's three woodpecker species is well distributed
across wooded areas of Wiltshire with strongholds in the woodlands of the
Avon Vale. This species nests in a drilled out hole, most often in a dead oak
or beech tree, and feeds mostly on insects or their larvae occupying dead
wood. They are also highly adaptable and are a common site at garden
birdfeeders in many urban gardens.

TAWNY OWL *Strix aluco*, OWLETS REST IN AN OAK TREE **(ABOVE)**
BROADTOWN
PHILIP MALE

The commonest Wiltshire owl most often inhabits broad leaved and mixed woodland, but also farmland hedgerows and parks. Identified by the classic 'to-wit-too-woo', this owl feeds on small mammals, mice and voles, but also beetles and sometimes small birds.

SPARROWHAWK *Acciptier nisus* **(RIGHT)**
BROADTOWN
PHILIP MALE

An elusive and secretive raptor, most often seen in a flash or evidenced by coming across a recent kill and flurry of feathers on the ground. While mostly a woodland species, the sparrowhawk has adapted well to urban gardens with lots of tree cover, where plenty of prey occur. The sparrowhawk commonly feeds on tits and finches but will also take larger wood pigeons and collared doves.

BRISTOL AVON (LEFT)
BRISTOL AVON, BELOW WIDBROOK WOOD NEAR TROWBRIDGE
STEPHEN DAVIS

The Bristol Avon rises in the north west of the county near Sherston, increasing in size and flow as it passes through the towns of Malmesbury, Chippenham and Melksham on its way to Bradford-on-Avon. A clay river, prone to flash flooding, water levels can rise rapidly by several metres. Water lilies *Nuphar lutea* characterise the low flows. The river is home to many dragonfly species.

GREY WAGTAIL *Motacilla cinerea* **(ABOVE)**
RIVER MARDEN, CALNE
PHILIP MALE

This species is most often associated with fast flowing streams and rivers. They are very active birds, searching for their insect prey on or near water and the damp edges of river banks. They classically bob up and down, and 'wag' their tails during this searching activity.

The Marlborough Downs and Savernake Forest

The Marlborough Downs form a high undulating chalk plateau, which falls away to the northwest, affording wide views over the lower chalk plateau and the clay vale, Swindon and beyond. To the south of the downs lies the Vale of Pewsey. The Ridgeway long distance footpath, itself an ancient track, follows the line of the higher chalk scarp and continues eastwards along the chalk out of the county. The landscape is characterised by large, open arable fields with small beech clumps on hilltops and tumuli. Its open aspect is accentuated by a sparse population of isolated farms, hamlets and a few villages nestling in dry valleys. Horse gallops and race horse breeding lie alongside the more usual arable farming.

Within these downs are dry valleys, with a surface scattering of sarsen stones which have been used over millennia, not only for stone circles but for all manner of building uses, from gateposts to church foundations. The sarsen stones are natural exposures of harder sandstone which have been weathered over the centuries to their present distinctive shapes. A local, alternative name is wethers (an old word for castrated rams), as particularly on misty, winter days, the stones resemble grey sheep when seen from a distance. Fyfield Down, between Avebury and Marlborough, has a large concentration of sarsen stones which support rare lichens and mosses.

Sheep and cattle graze the valley sides as they have done for thousands of years. The flower rich grasslands are protected as Sites of Special Scientific Interest, at Pewsey Downs and Fyfield Down National Nature Reserves. The Trust's nature reserves at Morgan's Hill, Ham Hill and High Clear Down are particularly species rich. Prominent on the western edge above Devizes is Roundway Down hill fort where restoration of grazing has promoted an abundance of wild flowers.

Tan Hill, together with the adjacent Milk Hill, are the highest points in Wiltshire, where they overlook the Pewsey Vale. Herbaceous plants, such as wild thyme, common rockrose, field scabious and restharrow are abundant. Scattered scrub provides shelter for corn buntings, yellowhammers and linnets. Within the Marlborough Downs are woods with ancient oaks and stands of beech, and vibrant scented carpets of spring bluebells. The largest wood which contains many different habitats is Savernake Forest. Many of the largest oaks have been given names such as, the saddle oak, spider oak, king oak and big belly oak, reflecting their antiquity and characteristic varied shapes. In the north west the Trust manages Clouts Wood nature reserve with its rich plant and bird life, just to the south of Wroughton.

WINTER SUNRISE
AVEBURY STONE CIRCLE
STEPHEN DAVIS

The world's largest pre-historic stone circle, Avebury, is part of the Stonehenge and Avebury World Heritage Site, an outstanding Neolithic and Bronze Age monumental landscape. These dramatic monuments are long known to have been built in synchrony with the movements of the earth's path around the sun.

RIVER WATER CROWFOOT *Ranunculus aquatilis* (ABOVE)
RIVER KENNET, FYFIELD
ROBERT HARVEY

The River Kennet is a nationally important chalk stream, flowing through the Marlborough Downs from its headwaters near Silbury Hill, through the county into Berkshire and on to the River Thames. Its crystal clear waters flow as surface groundwater from the chalk aquifer below ground.

WILD GARLIC *Allium ursinum* (RIGHT)
CLOUTS WOOD NATURE RESERVE
STEPHEN DAVIS

Clouts Wood is situated on the steep chalk escarpment above the village of Wroughton. A traditional coppice woodland of largely ash *Fraxinus excelsior* and field maple *Acer campestre*, with many oak standards. Aspen *Populus tremulus* and common lime *Tilia* x *europaea* also occur. The ground flora supports many ancient woodland indicators such as wild garlic *allium ursinum*, green hellebore *Helleborus viridis* and bath asparagus *Ornithogalum pyrenaicum*.

ANCIENT OAK, WINTER *Quercus robur* **(LEFT)**
SAVERNAKE FOREST
STEPHEN DAVIS

Savernake Forest is host to a large number of ancient oak trees. The largest are thought to be more than one thousand years old. Many are multi-stemmed, evidence of the historic practice of pollarding.

WINTER LANDSCAPE (ABOVE)
PEWSEY DOWNS NATIONAL NATURE RESERVE
STEPHEN DAVIS

Occasionally snow comes to Wiltshire transforming the landscape, as here looking across the ridges of chalk and the Pewsey Vale towards Salisbury Plain in the distance. Thousands of anthills and the parallel tracks of grazing livestock traverse the downland slopes. Woodborough Hill and Picked Hill in the distance, are outliers of chalk geology which rise above the greensand of the Pewsey Vale.

PURPLE EMPEROR *Apatura iris* **(ABOVE)**
SAVERNAKE FOREST
STEVE COVEY

This striking butterfly is the 'emperor' of the forest. It breeds on common
sallow *Salix caprea* bushes occurring in woodland rides and the edges of
clearings. It has a powerful rapid gliding flight. It spends much of its time
in the tree canopy where males set up territories in search of a mate. Males
descend to the woodland floor and take up moisture and minerals from
damp track surfaces, and also from animal dung.

GREAT GREEN BUSH CRICKET *Tettigonia viridissima* **(RIGHT)**
ROUNDWAY DOWN, DEVIZES
ROBERT HARVEY

The largest cricket in the UK, occurs in rough grassland and scrub. The
female requires patches of bare soil in which she lays her eggs.

MEADOW SAFFRON *Colchicum autumnale* (**LEFT**)
MARKHAM BANKS, WROUGHTON
STEPHEN DAVIS

Despite being no relation to the true crocus the flowers of meadow saffron are deceptively similar, the primary difference being the presence of six stamens (the pollen-producing reproductive organ of a flower) to the true crocus's three. A much overlooked and declining plant of meadows and woods it occurs in only a few places in Wiltshire, such as here at Markham Banks.

FRAGRANT ORCHIDS *Gymnadenea conopsea* (**ABOVE**)
PEWSEY DOWNS NATIONAL NATURE RESERVE
STEPHEN DAVIS

The chalk downs support many species of orchid amongst a very diverse flora. Drifts of fragrant orchids occur on the banks of ancient trackways which descend the scarp slope.

SILBURY HILL **(ABOVE)**
STONEHENGE AND AVEBURY WORLD HERITAGE SITE
PHIL SELBY

At 4,400 years old Silbury Hill is the largest pre-historic mound in Europe. Despite extensive excavations its original purpose remains a mystery.

LONE BEECH, SUMMER SUNSET **(RIGHT)**
ROUNDWAY HILL FORT
STEPHEN DAVIS

This beech tree stands on the edge of Oliver's Castle on Roundway Down, an early Iron Age hill fort named after Oliver Cromwell. The Battle of Roundway Down was fought here on 13th July 1643, during the first English Civil War, when the Royalist Cavalry defeated the Parliamentarians.

SILBURY HILL WINTER SUNRISE
STONEHENGE AND AVEBURY WORLD HERITAGE SITE
STEPHEN DAVIS

Situated close to the headwaters of the River Kennet, the ground water
rises in winter in response to rainfall, to create a circular moat at the base of
the hill.

RIVER KENNET WINTER FLOOD
WEST OVERTON
STEPHEN DAVIS

Pollarded willows reflect in the flooded River Kennet. Water levels in the river rise as ground water fills the chalk aquifer below. This can cause localised flooding in the upper reaches of the river. Conversely, in periods of drought, the upper reaches of the Kennet can dry up as ground water levels drop.

SPRING BEECH *Fagus sylvatica*
SAVERNAKE FOREST
STEPHEN DAVIS

Alongside the ancient oaks are large numbers of ancient beech pollards.
These multi-stemmed trees often tower above the rest of the canopy and
are particularly attractive in early spring.

BLUEBELL SUNRISE
WEST WOODS
STEPHEN DAVIS

In the large beech plantation to the west of Marlborough the ground flora is dominated by bluebells *Hyacinthoides non-scriptus* in spring. Other ancient woodland indicators include, wild daffodil *Narcissus pseudonarcissus* and Solomon's-seal *Polygonatum multiflorum.*

TWISTED OAK *Quercus robur* (**LEFT**)
SAVERNAKE FOREST
STEPHEN DAVIS

Many of the ancient oak trees in Savernake Forest are twisted and contorted, with branches of greater diameter than any young oak growing in the wider forest. These old trees support many fungi and insect species, and offer up holes and cracks for nesting birds and roosting bats.

AUTUMN BEECH *Fagus sylvatica* (**ABOVE**)
SAVERNAKE FOREST
STEPHEN DAVIS

Savernake Forest is at least 1000 years old. The Forest is referred to in a Saxon Charter from King Athelstan in 934AD, as 'Safernoc'. The great beech avenues of Savernake Forest were planted by 'Capability Brown' in the 1740s on the instruction of Lord Thomas Bruce.

SARSEN STONES
LOCKERIDGE DENE
ROBERT HARVEY

The Sarsen stones of Lockeridge Dene became a protected landscape in 1908. These huge sandstone blocks, preserved here, and at Pigledene and Fyfield Down, used to litter the Kennet valley and the Marlborough Downs. They were used for the construction of Avebury stone circle and Stonehenge, twenty miles to the south, and were used extensively for building as recently as the early twentieth century. A geologically significant landscape, the Sarsen stones also support rare lichen species.

ROUNDWAY DOWN
ROUNDWAY DOWN
STEPHEN DAVIS

These dramatic folds in the chalk mark the western boundary of the North Wessex Downs Area of Outstanding Natural Beauty. The many visible shallow ridges which traverse the slopes of the chalk escarpment are the result of years of stock grazing with cattle and sheep. The slopes of the downs are covered in wildflowers in spring and summer.

The Vale of Pewsey

The Vale of Pewsey is a gently undulating greensand valley which separates the Marlborough Downs from Salisbury Plain. The market town of Devizes lies at the western edge of the valley, where the Caen Hill lock flight descends to the Avon Vale. Relatively steep, rounded and folded chalk scarps form the northern and southern boundaries. Within the Vale are arable fields, along with pastures and meadows on the damper soils in the valley bottom. This vale is traditionally an area of dairy farms with discrete small villages and outlying farms.

As with many of the other living landscapes of Wiltshire, the Vale has been continuously farmed for millennia. Within living memory, hedgerows have been dug up to make room for larger, more productive, fields with wet woodlands cleared and drained. Some farmers and landowners have resisted large scale changes and others are now actively replanting hedgerows, fruit trees, shelter belts and field margins in an effort to rebuild and increase wildlife.

The headwaters of the Salisbury River Avon rise as springs at Jones's Mill nature reserve, where an area of valley fen and mire survives as a unique remnant of unimproved and undrained land. The fen here is a national stronghold for Desmoulin's whorl snail.

The greater tussock sedge echoes a more ancient landscape. Cotton grass and bog pimpernel, otherwise rare in Wiltshire, occur within the mire, as do large drifts of marsh marigold, meadow sweet and southern marsh orchids.

The Kennet and Avon canal was built during the late 18th and early 19th centuries. As well as helping with transportation for local trade, it brought new building materials, such as Welsh roofing slates, to complement the traditional thatch. Originally the canal would have been as alien, contentious and invasive in the landscape as a new motorway or railway is today. The canal has long since melded into the landscape and is an important wildlife corridor. It is also home for many people living on narrowboats, as well as providing diverse and sustainable recreation on the water and along the banks.

The small reserve of Peppercombe Wood lies on the edge of Urchfont village beside and overlooking a gently hilly area of pasture fields. In this area the tracks and roadways have cut through the relatively soft greensand, leaving holloways or sunken lanes with trees arching to form a natural roof high above.

CORN STOOKS NEAR MARDEN
MARDEN
STEPHEN DAVIS

A few farms in the vale near the villages of Marden and Patney grow long stemmed thatching straw.

MARSH FRITILLARY BUTTERFLIES *Euphydryas aurinia*
PEWSEY DOWNS NATIONAL NATURE RESERVE
STEPHEN DAVIS

Wiltshire is a national stronghold for the marsh fritillary butterfly.
Populations naturally fluctuate in response to climate, but also through
its relationship with a small wasp parasite. Occasionally, in favourable
conditions the population can explode with many thousands of individuals
emerging on a single site.

MARSH MARIGOLD *Caltha palustris*
DREWS POND WOOD LOCAL NATURE RESERVE, DEVIZES
STEPHEN DAVIS

Marsh marigold is abundant in an area of peaty fen vegetation beside a small stream at Drews Pond Wood, growing amongst alder *Alnus glutinosa* trees. Such wet woodland habitat is now very scarce. This small wood supports twenty nine plant species indicative of ancient woodland.

APRIL SUNRISE **(ABOVE)**
VIEW FROM WALKERS HILL, PEWSEY DOWNS ESCARPMENT
STEPHEN DAVIS

The southern edge of the Marlborough Downs extends from Roundway Down in the west, above Devizes, to Martinsell Hill in the east.

MIST LAYERS PEWSEY VALE **(RIGHT)**
MARTINSELL HILL
PHIL SELBY

The eastern end of the Pewsey Vale captures the mist in autumn and winter. This is an intimate landscape of small woodland copses, hedgerows, arable fields and pasture.

APRIL SUNRISE
VIEW FROM KNAPP HILL, PEWSEY DOWNS ESCARPMENT
STEPHEN DAVIS

Looking across the vale towards Salisbury Plain, from Knap Hill on the
Pewsey Downs above Alton Barnes.

DAWN SHADOWS ON THE MIST
MARTINSELL HILL
STEPHEN DAVIS

In winter the low sun rises to the south east above Salisbury Plain, casting
dramatic shadows across the Vale.

WOODBOROUGH HILL SPRING MISTS
WOODBOROUGH HILL
STEPHEN DAVIS

Woodborough Hill stands as an outlier of chalk above the Pewsey Vale.
Topped by a small woodland copse, species rich chalk grassland occurs
on the thin chalky soils in the fields below.

SUNRISE
CAEN HILL LOCK FLIGHT, DEVIZES
STEPHEN DAVIS

Situated on the Kennet and Avon canal, the Caen Hill lock flight rises 237ft
in two miles, as it ascends through twenty seven separate locks, from the
bottom to the top at Devizes. The canal extends from Bristol through to
Reading where it joins the Thames. In September the sun rises directly
through a gap at the top of the main flight of sixteen locks.

AUTUMN IN THE VALE
ALTON BARNES
KEN LESLIE

Autumn sun lights the Vale from above Alton Barnes. This is the location of
a neolithic long barrow, now aptly named Walkers Hill, situated in the heart
of Pewsey Downs National Nature Reserve.

AUTUMN MISTS AT SUNRISE
MARTINSELL HILL
STEPHEN DAVIS

Eastwick Farm nestles at the head of the Pewsey Vale just below Martinsell
hill fort. The north facing escarpment of Salisbury Plain is seen in the
distance.

DAWN MIST
JONES'S MILL NATURE RESERVE
STEPHEN DAVIS

This nationally important area of natural fen vegetation occurs in a shallow valley mire, at the headwaters of the River Avon, to the north east of Pewsey. Characteristic plants include, marsh valerian *Valeriana dioica*, greater tussock sedge *Carex paniculata* and meadowsweet *Filipendula ulmaria*. Fifty breeding bird species have been recorded on the reserve including sedge warbler *Acrocephalus schoenobaenus* and reed bunting *Emberiza schoeniclus*. Snipe *Gallinago gallinago* regularly use the reserve.

GREEN-WINGED ORCHIDS *Orchis morio* **(LEFT)**
WOODBOROUGH HILL
STEPHEN DAVIS

The nationally scarce green-winged orchid occurs in abundance in the grassland on the slopes of Woodborough Hill.

BLUEBELLS *Hyacinthoides non-scriptus* **AND OLD OAK COPPICE (ABOVE)**
GOPHER WOOD, HUISH
STEPHEN DAVIS

Sitting above the Pewsey Vale, this ancient woodland occurs on the scarp slope of the Pewsey Downs above the small village of Huish. Gopher Wood is mix of oak *Quercus robur*, ash *Fraxinus excelsior*, filed maple *Acer campestre* and hazel *Corylus avellana*. The wood supports a rich ground flora, with drifts of blue bells and wild garlic *Allium ursinum* in spring.

Salisbury Plain

The Plain is about the size of the Isle of Wight. It is the greatest unbroken expanse of chalk grassland in Europe. It lies south of the Vale of Pewsey and stretches down to the River Wylye and Salisbury. Salisbury Plain is home to the British Army's largest training area. The Army first started training towards the end of the 19th century. Consequently large swathes of land have escaped both intensive 20th century farming methods and urban development. This has conserved a wildlife rich landscape, which is unrivalled in lowland Britain, indeed Europe.

The wide open, grassy plains of the restricted areas with their small clumps of woodland, scattering of shrubs, including junipers, give a sense of stepping back in time. Porton Down in particular supports a rich, short-grazed turf covered in thyme, rock rose, squinancywort and ladies bedstraw, with many typical downland butterflies in great abundance, such as chalkhill blue, brown argus and dark green fritillary.

Birdsong fills the sky in early summer, skylarks are joined periodically by the call of the rare stone curlew, corn bunting and yellow hammer. Stonechat, whinchat and wheatear are also common. Barn owls are a frequent sight, feeding on the large vole population, as are short-eared owls in winter. The Plain is home to many birds of prey, including the graceful Montagu's harrier in summer, and the rare hen harrier in winter. Peregrine falcon, merlin, buzzard, kestrel and increasingly the red kite are regularly seen. The most striking bird of the Plain is the great bustard which became extinct in Britain in 1832. It has recently been re-introduced to the Plain using birds from Russia and Spain.

Besides using the area for training, the Army undertakes scrub management and clearance and allows tenant farmers to graze extensive areas of grassland. The Trust manages nature reserves at Cockey Down and the Devenish Reserve in the Woodford valley.

The Plain is home to many ancient monuments, the most famous being the Stonehenge stone circle. Around it and further afield are many more Neolithic earthworks. Old Sarum, the hillfort overlooking Salisbury was used by the Romans and Saxons, and subsequently the Normans, who built a castle and cathedral surrounding town. Old Sarum was the precursor of New Sarum, the City of Salisbury, founded in the 13th century in the valley below.

The great dome of chalk that constitutes Salisbury Plain is undulating in nature, with many sheltered chalk valleys. In these valleys, winterbournes rise as surface level springs, before flowing on to join the larger River Avon as it flows south through Wiltshire down to the coast.

STONEHENGE STAR TRAIL
STONEHENGE AND AVEBURY WORLD HERITAGE SITE
ROBERT HARVEY

Perhaps the world's most famous prehistoric monument, the Stonehenge stone circle occurs towards the southern edge of Salisbury Plain. Set amongst chalk downland, it was built about 5000 years ago, erected using Sarsen stones brought from the Marlborough Downs. It is long thought of to be an astronomical calender aligned with the sun and stars.

COMMON ROCKROSE **(ABOVE)**
SIDBURY HILL
STEPHEN DAVIS

A carpet of common rockrose *Helianthemum nummularium* can dominate the chalk grassland sward, often under the influence of rabbit grazing in addition to livestock grazing. Here common rockrose has colonised, ten years after the restoration and clearance of extensive conifer plantations, on the slopes of Sidbury Hill iron age hill fort to the north of Tidworth.

WINCHAT *Saxicola rubetra* **(RIGHT)**
SALISBURY PLAIN
JAMES FISHER

Breeding winchat are almost exclusively confined to the Salisbury Plain Training Area which holds the most significant population in lowland England. Mostly seen in the unimproved grasslands of the dry chalk valleys, this species overwinters in sub-saharan Africa.

STARLING MURMURATION AND PEREGRINE FALCON *Falco peregrinus*
SALISBURY PLAIN
STEPHEN DAVIS

Starlings gather in large communal roosts in the winter months.
Supplemented by birds from Europe, the largest roosts hold more than a
million birds. Starling murmurations are a spectacular sight when the flock is
seen to dance and swirl in a magical unison, before descending to roost at
dusk. This is most often stimulated by the presence of a bird of prey, such
as here by a peregrine falcon.

GRAZING SHEEP AND STARLINGS *Sturnus vulgaris*
SALISBURY PLAIN
JAMES FISHER

Large flocks of sheep are grazed extensively on Salisbury Plain. Flocks of
starlings follow the sheep, feeding on insects disturbed by the livestock.
Salisbury Plain has been grazed extensively for thousands of years and
survives as the largest remaining contiguous block of chalk grassland in the
UK, which once extended from Dorset through to the Chilterns.

RAINBOW
SALISBURY PLAIN
GARY MANTLE

The extensive grasslands of Salisbury Plain cover almost twenty thousand hectares. This represents the largest remaining area of chalk grassland in western Europe and is a uniquely important habitat for a great diversity of wildlife.

WESTBURY WHITE HORSE
SALISBURY PLAIN
ROBERT HARVEY

The oldest of Wiltshire's white horses occurs on a steep west facing slope on the escarpment of Salisbury Plain. Situated below the Iron Age hillfort called Bratton Camp, it enjoys spectacular panoramic views across the western Pewsey vale. The origins of this figure are obscure, though there has been a figure here for at least 300 years.

GREAT BUSTARDS *Otis tarda*
SALISBURY PLAIN
GARY MANTLE

The great bustard is the county bird of Wiltshire, appearing on the crest of the county coat of arms and flag. Formerly it was present across the wide open chalk grasslands of Salisbury Plain, common enough to grace the Mayoral banquet table. The great bustard has recently been re-introduced back to Salisbury Plain from populations in both Russia and Spain.

PYRAMIDAL ORCHIDS *Anacamptis pyramidalis*
NEAR TILSHEAD, SALISBURY PLAIN
STEPHEN DAVIS

Drifts of pyramidal orchids can be seen on some of our road verges where
chalk soils are present. Managed sensitively road verges are vital corridors
linking ecological networks together.

MARSH FRITILLARY *Euphydryas aurinia*
SALISBURY PLAIN
STEPHEN DAVIS

Wiltshire is a national (and European) stronghold for this species. Perhaps
the largest colony in Europe occurs on Salisbury Plain. This species breeds
on devils bit scabious *Succisa pratensis* in medium length turf (10-20 cms).
In Wiltshire it favours chalk downland, with one or two isolated colonies
occurring in rough pastures which are rich in the foodplant.

RED BACKED SHRIKE *Lanius collurio*
SALISBURY PLAIN
STEVE COVEY

Once a regular sight in Wiltshire and lowland England, this species is
now only a rare migrant visitor to the county. The entire world population
overwinters in east and southern Africa.

RIVER WATER CROWFOOT *Ranunculus aquatilis* AND HEMLOCK WATER DROPWORT *Oenanthe fistulosa* **(LEFT)**
RIVER AVON
STEPHEN DAVIS

The River Avon, along with its tributaries, the chalk streams of the Wylye, Nadder and Ebble, is the most species rich riverine ecosystem in the UK. It supports more specialist plant and fish species than any other chalk stream.

PEREGRINE FALCON *Falcao peregrinus* **(ABOVE)**
RIVER AVON
JAMES FISHER

Peregrine falcons are continuing to recover from an historical low point, in Wiltshire and nationally, following both persecution and the impact of organochlorine pesticides. Regularly feeding on starlings and pigeons, they are also known to take golden plover *Pluvialis apricaria* and common teal *Anas crecca* in the Cotswold Water Park in north Wiltshire.

West Wiltshire Downs and the Vale of Wardour

The chalk downs lying south of Salisbury Plain and the Wylye valley stretch down towards the southern county border and into Dorset. They encompass areas of open downland and woodlands on the high ridges, such as Grovely Woods, Great Ridge and Cranbourne Chase (once a royal hunting Forest). Earthworks of ancient barrows and hillforts are scattered over the landscape, with wide open skies and extensive views. Today there are a few farms and agricultural buildings up on the downs but most of the population lives in the sheltered valleys. The tops of the downs have large arable fields, originally created from 18th and 19th century enclosures and made larger by 20th century intensive farming.

Large and smaller wooded areas consist of ancient semi-natural woodlands. Small copses and shelter belts, often of beech and oak, follow the contours of the hills. Within the woodlands there are sheltered arable and pasture fields which are often linked to the woods by hedgerows containing mature trees. One small wood comprises old yews forming a distinctly different habitat. These evergreen trees produce berries which support flocks of birds during the winter months, such as greenfinches, bullfinches, fieldfares and redwings. This area is a stronghold for farmland birds. Species rich chalk grasslands have survived on the steep scarp slopes and valley sides of a series of parallel dry chalk valleys and hill forts. They have escaped intensive farming and remain flower and invertebrate rich habitats sustaining a rich bird life. The areas of unimproved chalk downland are largely islands within an otherwise intensively farmed landscape. Connectivity between these blocks is beginning to improve through environmental stewardship schemes and the reversion of some arable land back to chalk grassland.

At Coombe Bissett Down nature reserve the Trust has restored arable land back to flower rich downland. Grazing with Dexter cattle follows traditional patterns and hay is sometimes cut after plants have flowered and seeded, depending on the season.

The rivers Ebble and Nadder both flow quietly through this chalk landscape, feeding into the River Avon at Salisbury. They are beautiful chalk streams, rich in wildlife including brown trout, salmon, otter and water vole.

HINDON DROVE
BROADCHALKE
ANDREW WILTSHIRE

The West Wiltshire Downs are traversed by many historic droves and ancient byways, along which farmers would move their livestock, cattle and sheep to and from markets. These were essential trading routes.

AUTUMN MIST
MARLEYCOMBE
KEN LESLIE

Autumn mists fill the dry chalk valleys which incise the Downs.

AUTUMN GRAZING
MARLEYCOMBE
KEN LESLIE

Cattle have grazed the downland slopes for centuries. The activity of grazing over the years has produced the many parallel terraces that traverse the slopes. Grazing is an essential farming activity to maintain the species rich sward.

SPRING OAK TREE AND BLUEBELLS *Hyacinthoides non-scriptus* **(ABOVE)**
ASHMORE
KEN LESLIE

The ancient woodlands of the Cranborne Chase have an unbroken history of management. Cranborne Chase has its origins as an ancient hunting forest. It includes remnants of enclosed medieval coppice, common land, wood pasture and more recent hazel plantations. Drifts of bluebells carpet the woodland floor in spring.

BARN OWL *Tyto alba* **(RIGHT)**
LANGFORD LAKES NATURE RESERVE, WYLYE VALLEY
JAMES FISHER

The barn owl is crepuscular in habit, often seen hunting at the margins of the day, dawn and dusk, as here lit by the early dawn light over Great Meadow. This is an area of recently restored wet grassland in the Wylye valley at Langford Lakes.

WINTER HOAR FROST (ABOVE)
MIDDLETON DOWN NATURE RESERVE
KEN LESLIE

Winter frosts can be severe on the Downs, as here at the Trust's nature reserve south of Broadchalke.

SPRING (RIGHT)
BISHOPSTONE MEADOWS RIVER EBBLE
KEN LESLIE

The River Ebble is a gently flowing chalk stream, a tributary of the River Avon. It flows through the Ebble Valley, from its headwaters near Berwick St John, through to the Avon which it joins just to the south of Salisbury.

COWSLIPS *Primula veris* (LEFT)
BROADCHALKE
ANDREW WILTSHIRE

Cowslips are one of the first spring flowers to appear on the Downs in early spring emerging in April, often alongside the first orchids of the season, the early purple orchid *Orchis mascula*. On the chalk downs they can occur in great abundance. They are purported to have a delicate smell of apricots and are the foodplant of the rare Duke of Burgundy *Hamearis lucina* butterfly.

DAWN OVER BOWERCHALKE (ABOVE)
BOWERCHALKE
ANDREW WILTSHIRE

The Downs above Bowerchalke are rich in wildflowers. Meadow saxifrage *Saxifraga granulata* is abundant here. It is otherwise a rare plant in Wiltshire confined to a very few chalk downs and neutral meadows.

COW PARSLEY *Anthriscus sylvestris*
CHALKE VALLEY
ANDREW WILTSHIRE

More common plants such as the attractive lacy flowers of the cow parsley are characteristic of field margins, wood edges and roadside verges. They serve as valuable nectar sources for many plant pollinators and as connective corridors for insects and birds within the wider landscape.

CHURCH BOTTOM MIST
CHURCH BOTTOM
KEN LESLIE

Summer cattle grazing on the downs promotes wildflowers above the more
dominant grasses.

RIVER WYLYE FIRST LIGHT
RIVER WYLYE
KEN LESLIE

The River Wylye starts as a small stream in the west of the county near
Maiden Bradley. As it flows through the downland landscape of the Wylye
valley it broadens into a major river, before it joins with the River Nadder at
Wilton, and then onto Salisbury to finally join the Avon. The Wylye is part of
the most diverse chalk river system in the UK.

AUTUMN FONTHILL LAKE
FONTHILL LAKE
KEN LESLIE

Situated in the heart of the Cranborne Chase and West Wiltshire Downs
Area of Outstanding Natural Beauty, to the north of Tisbury, Fonthill lake
adds diversity to the landscape, in an area otherwise short of open water.

WHITESHEET HILL
LOOKING TOWARDS THE DEVERILLS
ANDREW WILTSHIRE

Whitesheet Hill is the site of a neolithic causewayed camp, a series of bronze age barrows and a large iron age hill fort. The slopes of these open chalk downs are host to a diverse downland flora, extensively grazed by sheep.

CHALKE VALLEY ABOVE NORRINGTON
EBBLE VALLEY
ANDREW WILTSHIRE

Extensive areas of chalk downland survive on the scarp slopes and valley
sides of the many dry coombes that characterise the Ebble Valley.

CHISELBURY RINGS (LEFT)
FOVANT
ANDREW WILTSHIRE

Chiselbury Rings encircle Chiselbury Camp, an iron age hill fort situated above the village of Fovant. It occupies a chalk ridge with commanding views over the Nadder valley to the north and the Ebble Valley to the south. The surrounding banked earthworks of this scheduled ancient monument are clothed in chalk downland flowers, including the sky blue small scabious *Scabiosa columbaria* and the delicate white flowers of burnett saxifrage *Pimpinella saxifrage*.

ANTHILL AND WILD THYME *Thymus serpyllum* (ABOVE)
LITTLE LANGFORD DOWN, WYLYE VALLEY
STEPHEN DAVIS

Little Langford Down nature reserve occupies a small north east facing valley surrounded by Grovely Wood on the edge of the Wylye Valley. It has an outstanding chalk downland flora with many ancient anthills created by the yellow meadow ant *Lasius flavius*. The activity of the ants creates a remarkable localised topography and micro-climate which favours the colonisation of warmth loving plants, such as wild thyme, common rockrose *Helianthemum nummularium* and ladies bedstraw *Galium verum*.

AUTUMN SHEEP AT DAWN
CRANBORNE CHASE DOWNS
KEN LESLIE

The elevated downlands of the Cranborne Chase are a place of big skies and solitude. Autumn and winter grazing by sheep prepares the sward for a new growth of wildflowers and fine grasses in the spring, and the return of cowslips, orchids and the myriad chalk downland herbs.

LADY'S BEDSTRAW *Galium verum*
COOMBE BISSETT DOWN NATURE RESERVE
STEPHEN DAVIS

Coombe Bissett Down near Salisbury is the centre of the Trust's southern farming operation hosting the Trust's herd of Dexter cattle and flock of Herdwick sheep. The reserve here continues to be expanded by the conversion of adjacent blocks of arable land back to chalk grassland rich in orchids and other wildflowers.

Tytherley and Langley Woods

To the south east of Salisbury the chalk gives way to two distinct areas of clay and sand. Tytherley Forest is an area of broadleaved mixed deciduous woodland, well known for its abundance of butterflies and moths. Further south is an area of mature ancient woodlands, meadows and heath, the northernmost tip of the New Forest. The land is slightly undulating with extensive broad-leaved and planted conifer woods, amongst pasture and arable fields. Hedges bound the fields, criss-crossing between the woodland, giving an enclosed feel to the landscape. Roads and lanes twist through the woods to connect the hidden villages.

Amongst the largest blocks of ancient woodland in the area are Bentley Wood, and Blackmoor Copse, a Wiltshire Wildlife Trust nature reserve. There was a period of largescale felling of broadleaved trees, including many mature oaks in Bentley Wood, in the 1950's. Blackmoor Copse was first established as a nature reserve in 1956 in order to protect the butterfly populations, in particular the purple emperor. Since the original felling and replantings, Bentley Wood has been managed sensitively. It remains the only woodland in the county where you can find five different species of fritillary butterfly alongside other scarce species, such as the Duke of Burgundy and white-letter hairstreak. The dormouse benefits from large areas of hazel coppice in the understory. The management of these woods continues as it has for centuries producing valuable timber products and maintaining wildlife rich habitats.

The New Forest National Park just extends into Wiltshire and contains some outstanding ancient woodlands, with very large oak trees and, unusually extensive stands of small-leaved lime. In places extensive conifer plantations have been planted on the more acidic sand and gravel soils, where heather occurs in the understory, and in forest glades.

Villages are strung around old commons traditionally used for grazing. Within the woods lie damp boggy areas which are becoming increasingly rare in southern England. The Trust's reserve at Landford Bog has sallows and birches together with lowland heath and bog habitats, which support rare plants such as common sundews and creatures such as raft spiders. The tough vegetation is grazed by Dexter cattle which helps to maintain the habitat.

SMALL PEARL-BORDERED FRITILLARY *Boloria selene*
BENTLEY WOOD
STEVE COVEY

Formerly ubiquitous amongst damper coppice woodlands in Wiltshire this species appears to be now confined to Bentley Wood and Blackmoor Copse in Wiltshire, where it breeds on common dog violet *Viola canina*. In common with other fritillary butterflies this species has declined dramatically due to changes in woodland management, and the lack of active coppicing.

CHIFF CHAFF *Phylloscopus collybita* (**ABOVE**)
BLACKMOOR COPSE
PHILIP MALE

This delightful summer migrant usually arrives in Wiltshire in March having overwintered in southern Europe, north or sub-Saharan Africa. It is widely distributed in Wiltshire and breeds wherever broadleaved or mixed woodland occurs with a thick understory of smaller trees and shrubs. While most birds migrate south in late autumn this species is known to overwinter in mild years.

REDSTART *Phoenicurus phoenicurus* (**RIGHT**)
REDLYNCH
STEVE DEELEY

This is a rather scarce summer visitor which occurs in open mature deciduous woodland, preferring extensive old oak and beech forests such as at Langley Woods and Savernake Forest. The mature ancient woodlands of the south east corner of the county are the stronghold for this species in Wiltshire.

SILVER-STUDDED BLUE *Plebejus argus*
LANDFORD BOG
STEPHEN DAVIS

This heathland butterfly species just sneaks into the south east corner of the county, occurring on the Trust reserve at Landford Bog and a few localised patches of heathland. Caterpillar food plants include heather *Calluna vulgaris* and bell heather *Erica cinerea*.

DORMOUSE *Muscardinus avellanarius*
BLACKMOOR COPSE
DAVID KJAER

Blackmoor Copse nature reserve supports a
healthy population of the rare dormouse. These
secretive mammals live in mixed broadleaved
woodland and hedgerows. They are arboreal in
nature, living and moving about the woodland
canopy, feeding on flowers and pollen in spring,
fruit in summer and nuts in autumn. They
hibernate for up to seven months of the year.

SILVER-WASHED FRITILLARY MALE *Argynnis paphia* (**ABOVE**)
BENTLEY WOOD
ROBERT HARVEY

The largest of the fritillary butterflies prefers semi-shaded woodland for breeding, but also requires open sunny glades and clearings, where its favoured nectar plants such as bramble *Rubus fruticosus* and marsh thistle *Cirsium palustre* occur. The male is a striking orange colour with expanded veins on its forewings containing sex pheromones.

FIRECREST *Regulus ignicapillus* (**RIGHT**)
BENTLEY WOOD
JAMES FISHER

The smallest of British breeding birds appears to be slowly establishing itself in the county, but is confined to a very few locations, with a concentration of records at Bentley Wood. A peak of no more than seventeen singing males has been recorded in a single summer in Wiltshire.

ANCIENT OAK *Quercus robur* **(LEFT)**
LANGLEY WOOD NATIONAL NATURE RESERVE
STEPHEN DAVIS

Langley Wood National Nature Reserve, near Redlynch, is an outstanding ancient woodland supporting a great diversity of woodland habitats, breeding birds and rare lichens which grow on the older trees.
Birds, otherwise rare in Wiltshire, such as hawfinch *Coccothraustes coccothraustes*, nightjar *Caprimulgus europaeus* and redstart *Phoenicurus phoenicurus* occur here. The reserve has a particularly high density of larger ancient oak trees and stands of small-leaved lime *Tilia cordata*.

STOAT *Mustela erminea* **(ABOVE)**
TYTHERLEY
JAMES FISHER

Stoats prefer open country with a mix of hedges, ditches and copses. They often turn completely white in winter, apart from the black tip to the tail. Feeding on small mammals, birds eggs and small birds, they can take prey significantly larger than themselves such as rabbit.

HAZEL COPPICE *Corylus avellana* AND BLUEBELLS *Hyacinthoides non-scripta*
BLACKMOOR COPSE NATURE RESERVE
STEPHEN DAVIS

Blackmoor Copse contains extensive areas of hazel coppice in the understory, below high forest containing many oak standards. The coppice areas are favoured by the scarce dormouse *Muscardinus avellanarius*.

MARSH FRITILLARY *Euphydryas aurinia*   Stephen Davis

BROWN ARGUS *Aricia aegestis*   Stephen Davis

WHITE ADMIRAL *Leminitis camilla*   Stephen Davis

WHITE ADMIRAL *Leminitis camilla*   Stephen Davis

GREEN-VEINED WHITE *Pieris napi*   Stephen Davis

ORANGE TIP *Anthocharis cardamines*   Stephen Davis

MARBLED WHITE *Melanargia galathea*   Robert Harvey

BROWN HAIRSTREAK *Thecla betulae*   Stephen Davis

PURPLE HAIRSTREAK *Favonius quercus*   Steve Covey

CHALKHILL BLUE *Lysandra coridon*   Steve Covey

HOLY BLUE *Celastrina argiolus*   Gill Cardy

DINGY SKIPPER *Erynnis tages*   Steve Covey

ADONIS BLUE *Pollyommatus bellargus*   Gary Mantle

MARBLED WHITE *Melanargia galathea*   Robert Harvey

RINGLET *Aphantopus hyperantus*   Stephen Davis

GREEN HAIRSTREAK *Callophrys rubi*   Steve Covey

WOOD ANEMONE *Anemone nemorosa* AND WILD DAFFODIL *Narcissus pseudonarcissus*

FORGETMENOT *Myostis sylvatica* AND DANDELION *Taraxacum officinale*

DROPWORT *Filipendula vulgaris*

SNAKE'S HEAD FRITILLARY *Fritillaria meleagris*

SNAKE'S HEAD FRITILLARY WHITE FORM *Fritillaria meleagris*

MARSH HELLEBORINE *Epipactis palustris*

PRIMROSE *Primula vulgaris*

MARSH MARIGOLD *Caltha Palustris*

LESSER CELANDINE *Ficaria ficaria*

WOOD ANEMONE *Anemone nemorosa*

COW PARSLEY *Anthriscus sylvestris* AND RED CAMPION *Silene dioica*

LADY'S BEDSTRAW *Galium Verum*

SQUINANCYWORT *Asperula cynanchica* AND THYME *Thymus serpyllum*

ROUND-HEADED RAMPION *Phyteuma orbiculare*

SPINY RESTHARROW *Ononis spinosa*

HAREBELL *Campanula rotundifolia*

Flower photographs Stephen Davis

Contributing Photographers

The publication of 'Wild Wiltshire' would not have been possible without the generous commitment and skill of the contributing photographers. All of them are Wiltshire based photographers passionate about the wildlife and landscapes of Wiltshire and Swindon. The Trust is enormously grateful to them all for allowing us to share their inspirational images.

David Blake www.wessexwildlife.co.uk

Gill Cardy

Steve Covey www.flickr.com/photos/od0man/

Stephen Davis www.stephendavisphotography.co.uk

Steve Deeley www.artofthewild.co.uk

James Fisher www.jfwildlife.co.uk

Robert Harvey www.robertharvey.net

David Kjaer www.davidkjaer.com

Ken Leslie www.kenleslie.co.uk

Philip Male www.flickr.com/photos/12820758@N04 pjmale57@gmail.com

Gary Mantle

Phil Selby www.flickr.com/photos/philselby/ philselby3@gmail.com

Andrew Wiltshire www.countrysidephotography.org

Acknowledgements

Wiltshire Wildlife Trust would like to thank and acknowledge the following for their commitment and support in helping the Trust produce Wild Wiltshire. Mike Hill and The Hills Group Limited for their generous sponsorship. All of the named photographers for their inspiring images. Gary and Anne Mantle for their insight and original text. Stephen Davis for project management, image sourcing and editing. Nick Otway for his wonderful design. Michael Moody for image colour management. Emma Chapman, Michele Gard, Sam Wilson, Dean Sherwin and Purgle Linham for their support, advice and proof reading. All private landowners for sharing and enabling access to the beautiful landscapes of Wiltshire and Swindon. All Wiltshire Wildlife Trust staff for their expertise in managing our nature reserves, and for sharing these with Trust members and the public.